Saint Maximilian Kolbe

Saint Maximilian Kolbe
Mary's Knight

Written by
Patricia Edward Jablonski, FSP

Illustrated by
Karen Ritz

Pauline
BOOKS & MEDIA
Boston

Library of Congress Cataloging-in-Publication Data

Jablonski, Patricia E.
    Saint Maximilian Kolbe : Mary's knight / written by Patricia Edward
Jablonski ; illustrated by Karen Ritz.
        p. cm. — (Encounter the saints series ; 10)
    ISBN 0-8198-7045-5 (pbk.)
    1. Kolbe, Maximilian, Saint, 1894–1941—Juvenile literature. 2. Christian
saints—Poland—Biography— Juvenile literature. [1. Kolbe, Maximilian,
Saint, 1894–1941. 2. Saints.] I. Ritz, Karen, ill. II. Title. III. Series.
    BX4700.K55 J33 2001
    282'.092—dc21
        2001000141

"P" and PAULINE are registered trademarks of the Daughters of Saint Paul.

Published by Pauline Books & Media, 50 Saint Pauls Avenue, Boston, MA
02130–3491

Printed in the U.S.A.

SMK KSEUSAHUDNHA8-251051 7045-5

www.pauline.org

Pauline Books & Media is the publishing house of the Daughters of Saint
Paul, an international congregation of women religious serving the Church
with the communications media.

6 7 8 9 10 11 12   19 18 17 16 15

ENCOUNTER THE SAINTS SERIES

Blesseds Jacinta and Francisco Marto
Shepherds of Fatima

Blessed James Alberione
Media Apostle

Blessed Pier Giorgio Frassati
Journey to the Summit

Journeys with Mary
Apparitions of Our Lady

Saint Anthony of Padua
Fire and Light

Saint Andre Bessette
Miracles in Montreal

Saint Bernadette Soubirous
And Our Lady of Lourdes

Saint Catherine Labouré
And Our Lady of the Miraculous Medal

Saint Clare of Assisi
A Light for the World

Saint Elizabeth Ann Seton
Daughter of America

Saint Faustina Kowalska
Messenger of Mercy

Saint Francis of Assisi
Gentle Revolutionary

Saint Gianna Beretta Molla
The Gift of Life

Saint Ignatius of Loyola
For the Greater Glory of God

Saint Joan of Arc
God's Soldier

Saint John Bosco
Champion for the Young

Saint John Paul II
Be Not Afraid

Saint Kateri Tekakwitha
Courageous Faith

Saint Martin de Porres
Humble Healer

Saint Maximilian Kolbe
Mary's Knight

Saint Pio of Pietrelcina
Rich in Love

Saint Teresa of Avila
Joyful in the Lord

Saint Thérèse of Lisieux
The Way of Love

Saint Thomas More
Courage, Conscience, and the King

For even more titles in the
Encounter the Saints series,
visit: www.pauline.org/EncountertheSaints

CONTENTS

THE RED AND THE WHITE

Yes. She was still there.

Raymond Kolbe pressed his hands to his eyes and rubbed hard. What was happening? Did he dare look again?

A gentle voice broke the stillness. "Do not be afraid, Raymond. I bring you two crowns. Will you accept them?"

The kindness in the Lady's voice melted the boy's fear into confidence. He uncovered his eyes and raised his head. The weavers' son was face to face with the Mother of God!

How beautiful she was! So much more beautiful than Raymond had ever imagined. He wished that all time would stop. He wanted to stay there forever—in the presence of the Blessed Virgin, whose motherly smile seemed to embrace him in a special act of love. But with a gentle insistence, Mary was holding out two crowns to him.

"The white crown means that you will always be pure," she explained; "the red, that you will die a martyr."

The ten-year-old grew serious as he studied the crowns. He definitely wanted to try to keep his heart free from sin. But martyrdom? That would mean giving up his life for his faith. He stole another glance at Mary. She was intently watching him. His thoughts raced on. *Martyrdom! Jesus died on the cross for me. How could I ever refuse him anything?* Raymond knew what his answer must be.

"My Mother," he replied in a trembling voice, "my holy Mother . . . I accept both crowns!"

The Blessed Virgin was very pleased. Her smile grew even more brilliant. Then, as silently as she had come, she was gone. The kneeling boy was alone again. His heart was pounding so hard that the echo of its thumping seemed to shake the walls of the church.

"Raymond, what are you doing there behind the cupboard?"

The unexpected call of his mother startled the boy to his feet. With a hasty puff, he extinguished the oil lamp flickering before the family shrine of Our Lady of Czestochowa. This was his chance. It had been days now

"I accept both crowns!"

since the visit of the Blessed Virgin, and he still hadn't told either of his parents about it. Glancing back at Mary's image, he whispered, "My Lady, help me to tell Mama—now."

A faint smile played at Mrs. Kolbe's lips as she waited for her son. More pronounced, though, were the wrinkles of worry that tightened her usually serene expression. Something was definitely wrong with Raymond. And she was going to find out what it was.

The boy finally emerged from the corner, his eyes puffy and red.

"You've been crying, haven't you," Mrs. Kolbe gently prodded. "Can we talk about what's wrong?"

Raymond didn't answer.

His mother made another attempt. "You know, I've noticed a change in you lately, Raymond, a change for the better. You're much more obedient than you used to be." Again Mrs. Kolbe waited for some reaction. But her son only stared at the floor. "I've also seen how much time you spend before the altar of Our Lady of Czestochowa," she went on. "I'm happy to see that you go there to pray. But since you've been crying, something must be bothering you. Don't you want to tell me about it?"

Still no response. Mrs. Kolbe decided to try another tactic. "Now Raymond, don't make me take back what I said about your being obedient. . . . Tell me everything!"

The boy suddenly broke down and began to sob. "Remember, Mama, how one day you asked me what would become of me because I'm so stubborn?"

Mrs. Kolbe thought for a moment, then nodded.

"Well that question really made me think about the way I'd been acting. I felt very sad, and from then on I tried to be better. And I went to pray more in front of the picture of the Blessed Mother." Raymond paused to catch his breath, then hurried on in an excited tone. "When I first went to pray in front of the Virgin's shrine, I asked her what would become of me."

Mrs. Kolbe blinked back the tears that were beginning to cloud her own eyes.

"I asked Mary a second time in church," Raymond continued, "and then. . . ." his voice dropped to a whisper, "she appeared to me!"

While his mother listened in awe, Raymond described all the details of the apparition. With his characteristic simplicity, he concluded, "Ever since that day, Mama, whenever we go to church, I feel that I'm not going with you and Papa, but with the Blessed Mother and Saint Joseph."

There! The truth was out. Raymond could relax. Amazed though she was, Mrs. Kolbe silently praised God for the miraculous favor he had shown her son. She couldn't doubt Raymond. She knew it wasn't like him to make up such stories. Even more, the change in his life proved that he was telling the truth.

Mrs. Kolbe later wrote, "From this time on, Raymond was never the same. He would often excitedly come to me, anxious to talk about his desire to become a martyr."

Raymond himself never again spoke directly about his meeting with the Mother of God. But he quietly became more dedicated to Mary. He realized that she was the Mother, Teacher, and Queen who would lead him to Jesus.

He would follow her.

LATIN TO THE RESCUE

The family into which Raymond had been born on January 8, 1894, was poor but hardworking. His parents, Maria and Jules Kolbe, were simple people. They patiently labored at their weaving trade ten hours a day in order to support their three sons, Francis, Raymond and Joseph. Two other sons, Valentine and Anthony, born after Joseph, had both died at an early age.

Raymond had a quick mind and enjoyed performing science experiments and inventing things. He would set up battlefields and plan out different strategies for his imaginary "enemies." The colorful Polish countryside around his hamlet of Pabianice also fascinated the boy. Like Saint Francis of Assisi, Raymond loved nature. He saw the goodness and beauty of God reflected in all of creation. He could spend hours on end planting trees or amusing himself with animals.

Since the Kolbe family was not very well off, Mrs. Kolbe, in addition to her weaving, used to take on extra jobs to help make ends meet. While she was at work, young Raymond was in charge of the kitchen. He became quite a good chef. In fact, Mrs. Kolbe used to proudly boast about the delicious surprises Raymond often prepared.

Because of the family's meager income, only Francis, the eldest of the boys, attended school. Like Joseph, Raymond had to stay home.

A simple errand would change everything. . . .

"Praised be Jesus Christ!" Raymond called as he bounded into the drugstore.

The gray-haired pharmacist smiled at the sound of the traditional greeting. "Now and forever. Amen!" he responded. "What can I do for you today, Raymond?"

"My mother sent me to pick up a prescription for her, Mr. Kotowski," the boy replied. "I need some *Vencon greca,*" he explained with a trace of pride.

Where had young Kolbe learned such perfect Latin? The druggist's curiosity was aroused. "What school do you go to?" he asked casually.

The boy's face reddened. Mr. Kotowski had touched a sensitive spot.

"Oh . . . ah . . . I don't go to school," came the embarrassed answer. "Only Francis does. Our parents can't afford the tuition for the three of us. It's expensive, you know."

"Then where did you learn Latin?" Mr. Kotowski questioned. "Your pronunciation is excellent."

"Father Jakowski teaches us at church."

The pharmacist's brow furrowed as he turned to take a bottle from the shelf. *Isn't it too bad to deprive Raymond of an education just because he can't pay the tuition? The boy has a quick mind and is obviously eager to learn. Something should be done.*

Mr. Kotowski cleared his throat before speaking. "Raymond, here's the prescription for your mother. Tell her that I also have a proposal to make. If your parents are willing, I'll tutor you in my home after work. This way, at the end of the year, you can also take the final school examinations with Francis. How does that sound?"

The boy was too excited to answer. He could only nod his approval. Grinning from ear to ear, Raymond dropped the prescription money on the counter, picked up his purchase and sped home. This was almost too good to be true!

Mr. and Mrs. Kolbe were grateful for the druggist's generous offer, and soon Raymond began his studies. He applied himself with so much diligence and effort that he not only caught up with his brother, but also passed his year-end examinations with very high grades. Seeing the progress Raymond was making, Mr. and Mrs. Kolbe made the sacrifice of enrolling him in school for the next semester. He was thrilled.

His classmates soon recognized something in Raymond Kolbe that made him stand out. It was hard, though, to pinpoint it. It wasn't just his quick mind, his friendly personality, or his readiness to help whenever he could. It was more than this. His friends may not have realized it, but the love of God was taking a firmer and firmer hold on Raymond. Jesus had a plan for him.

3

DECISIONS

"Blessed be God in his angels and in his saints. . . ."

Eucharistic Benediction was almost over. The priest reverently removed the sacred Host from the monstrance and returned It to the tabernacle. The golden tabernacle door slid silently back into place. The parish mission had come to a close.

Thirteen-year-old Raymond and his fifteen-year-old brother Francis sat anxiously in one of the front pews. In a few minutes they heard the soft clap of approaching sandals. Francis nudged Raymond. "Here comes Father now."

The priest, clad in a Franciscan habit with the familiar knotted cord around his waist, paused as he passed the boys. He motioned for them to follow him.

The three filed into the dimly lit sacristy.

"So, I've heard that you're interested in entering our order," Father Peregrine began pleasantly as he switched on a light.

The brothers spontaneously looked at each other. Who would be brave enough to speak first? The tension was too much for Raymond. "Yes, Father," he blurted out. "My brother and I want to become Franciscans—as soon as possible!"

Father Peregrine smiled. "And what brought you to such an important decision?"

It seemed as if Francis had silently elected Raymond to be their spokesman, so he would have to try and explain. "Well, Father, Francis and I've come every day this week to listen to you and the other priest preach our parish mission. You've done a lot of good here. You've encouraged people to receive the sacraments again. You've forgiven our sins. You've taught us about God and helped us to pray." Raymond hesitated. *Was he saying this right?* Francis nodded, and Raymond finished in a breathless rush of words. "When you said that you'd welcome any young men who wanted to consecrate themselves to the Lord, I felt a happiness inside me that I can't explain. My brother feels the same way. We want to dedicate our whole lives to serving God and his people—just as Saint Francis did and just as you're doing."

The Franciscan eyed the two boys with respect. "You know," he said kindly, "the life of a priest or brother isn't an easy one. Besides the many joys, Jesus will sometimes allow you to carry his cross, too."

This time it was Francis's turn to answer. "We've thought about that already, Father. We're ready to make sacrifices, aren't we, Ray?"

"Yes, we're ready!" Raymond seconded.

Father Peregrine rested his large hands on the boys' shoulders. "From what you've told me, I believe it is God's will that you join our Franciscan family. Return home now and prepare your things. It will be a long trip to Lwów where you must go to enter our minor seminary." Noticing Raymond's fidgeting feet the priest couldn't hold back a grin. "Pray well, boys," he added, "and try to stay calm!"

Raymond and Francis left the sacristy in a happy daze. They were on their way. The year was 1907.

Back at home they told everything to their parents. "This is wonderful news!" exclaimed Mr. Kolbe. "Your mother and I are very proud of you both."

"Will you come with us when it's time to go to Lwów?" Francis asked in an unsteady voice.

"Not all the way," replied Mr. Kolbe. "But I'll go far enough to make sure you get safely across the frontier and into Cracow. You'll be able to continue on from there."

The Kolbe brothers left for the Franciscan minor seminary some months later, in October. The train ride from Cracow to Lwów was a real adventure. They had never been away from their own village before, or ridden on anything but horses or farm wagons.

Their adventures continued at the seminary, where they even heard a radio broadcast for the first time.

"I've read all about radio and seen drawings of telegraph keys," said Raymond excitedly. "But this is great! Actual voices and music—not just the dots and dashes of Morse code!"

"It's hard to listen to, though, with all that crackling and scratching noise in the background," Francis complained.

"It won't be long before they figure out a way to correct that," Raymond assured. "You'll see."

The Kolbe boys' first three years of study at the minor seminary passed quickly.

Raymond's real genius in math and science amazed both his teachers and classmates. His mind never stopped churning out new ideas and inventions. In 1910, he even predicted that someone would fly to the moon one day. He was right, of course, but no one really believed him at the time.

The day when sixteen-year-old Raymond had to make a new decision was drawing closer. Should he enter the novitiate and continue on in the Franciscan life? Or should he return home?

He didn't know.

4

THE SIGN

Couldn't a man who's consecrated his life to God and the Blessed Virgin also be a soldier and serve his country? Of course! You don't have to be a priest or brother to serve God and his Mother. You only need to lead a good and honorable life. And a military career is certainly honorable. . . .

With his talents for planning and inventing, the temptation that he should be doing something *more* began to shake Raymond's faith in his religious vocation. *Maybe I'm meant to live a different kind of life*, he thought.

Raymond struggled with his doubts. One day in chapel he bowed his head to the floor before the statue of the Blessed Virgin. *I promise that I will go to battle for you, Mary*, he prayed in his heart. The young seminarian wasn't sure how he would do this, but it seems that he was actually considering enlisting in the Polish army.

Confusing thoughts continued to crowd his mind. If he was really meant to be a soldier, then he should leave the monastery.

He had to make his choice now, since it was time to begin his novitiate and prepare himself to make the vows of poverty, chastity and obedience.

Father Provincial, there's something I need to speak to you about. . . . There had to be a better way to say it. Raymond paced nervously up and down the corridor. As he finally turned toward the provincial superior's office, his sluggish steps reflected his deep inner struggle.

I'll have to tell him that I'm going home, he mused. *I can't be a good priest and a soldier at the same time.* The shrill ring of the doorbell interrupted his thoughts. Then he heard hurried footsteps. Raymond spun around to see an out-of-breath friar approaching. "Brother Raymond . . . your mother . . . is here to see you. . . . She's waiting . . . in the parlor."

Raymond felt a lump in his throat. This visit was so unexpected. He hoped nothing was wrong at home.

Mrs. Kolbe stood up when Raymond came in. "You look so well!" she exclaimed, hugging him tightly.

"So do you, Mama, so do you. Please, sit down."

Raymond took a seat beside his mother. She seemed genuinely excited.

"I just had to come and tell you the wonderful news in person, Raymond. Your brother Joseph has decided to follow in your footsteps and join you and Francis in the monastery."

"That is good news, Mama."

"But that's not all," Mrs. Kolbe continued, her eyes shining with joy. "Papa and I have decided to dedicate our whole lives to God now that you children are all grown up. Papa has already left for Cracow to join the Franciscan Fathers. And I came here to Lwów to stay with the Benedictine Sisters. Just think, Raymond, now our whole family is dedicated to God!"

Raymond was stunned. He could never tell his mother now that he'd been planning to leave the monastery.

Mrs. Kolbe began readjusting her hat, a sign that the visit was over. "I know you're busy, Raymond, so I'll be going now. Let's always pray for one another."

"Yes, Mama," Raymond wholeheartedly promised. "Always."

No sooner had Mrs. Kolbe left, than Raymond rushed to his provincial superior's

"Now our whole family is dedicated to God!"

office. His thoughts were keeping time with his feet. His mother's joy was something he would never forget. Her visit had been a clear sign of God's will, of Mary's will. Now he knew what he must do.

Raymond reached the office door. He knocked excitedly.

"Come in," invited a voice from the other side.

The young brother pushed open the door and leaned in. "Father, I have something important to ask you. Is now a good time?"

"Of course, Raymond. Let's talk."

Raymond pulled the door shut behind him. "Father," he said decisively, "I've come to ask your permission to enter the novitiate. I want to be a Franciscan priest—with all my heart and for all my life!"

5

To the City of St. Peter

Entering the novitiate was a special event. As a reminder that he was starting off on a whole new way of life, Raymond was given a new name. From that day on, he was to be called Brother Maximilian.

There was no doubt about it, Brother Maximilian was very intelligent and very talented. And even though he tried never to stand out or to appear special, his superiors recognized his potential. In 1912, a year after he made his first vows, they sent Maximilian to Rome, Italy, to study at the famous Gregorian University.

The months flew by. Autumn cooled into winter. Brother Maximilian continued to study as hard as he could. He knew that this was what God was asking of him.

"What do you think of that new Polish friar?"

"Do you mean Maximilian, Maximilian Kolbe?"

"Yes. Yes, that's him. Having that young man in class is the closest I'll ever come to working with a genius. His mind never stops!"

"You're right. But do you know what else I've noticed about him? In spite of his intelligence, he's very humble and obedient. He never looks down on his classmates. Instead, he's always ready to help. . . ."

The talk continued among Brother Maximilian's professors. For his part, Maximilian was happy. He had always enjoyed school, but this opportunity to study more about God was a special privilege.

On November 1, 1914, the Feast of All Saints, Brother Maximilian again approached the altar, this time to make his perpetual vows. The chapel was hushed as one by one the friars offered the gift of their young lives to God and to his Church.

Brother Maximilian felt very close to heaven that day. Jesus, his Divine Master, rewarded his generosity by flooding his soul with a great peace and happiness, which no one or nothing could ever take from him. From then on, Maximilian grew even more in his special love for Mary.

It was already 1917, and World War I had been raging for three years.

"Brothers, let's all pray and offer many sacrifices for the intentions of our Holy Father," urged Maximilian's superior in a tired voice. "Only God knows how much he's suffering because of this terrible war."

It was easy to feel close to the anguished Pope Benedict XV, who lived nearby in Vatican City. Maximilian made up his mind then and there to take his superior's plea to heart.

The old refectory door creaked shut behind him. Brother Maximilian wasted no time. He was already on his way to talk things over with the One who could solve every problem—Jesus, living and present in the Holy Eucharist.

The monastery chapel was empty. Maximilian made an unhurried genuflection. The sun's last rays, still filtering through the stained glass, clothed his kneeling figure in a mist of ruby and amber. Brother Maximilian fixed his eyes on the tabernacle. He began to pour out his heart to the Lord. "Jesus," he prayed, "see how evil men are threatening the lives of your people and your Church with this war. Day after day, not only thousands of lives, but also thousands of souls are possibly being lost. Help me, Jesus. Please inspire me to do something for these souls, to conquer them all for you! May Mary, your Immaculate Mother and my Mother, too, intercede for me."

The drone of a distant fighter-bomber broke into his prayer. Hadn't he always been a soldier at heart? Yes. And somehow he was beginning to feel that he had been chosen by God to fight a special battle. The idea was still very confused in his mind. Brother Maximilian wasn't worried, though. God would let him know his will when the time came. As he had first done so many years before, Maximilian again placed his life in the hands of the Blessed Mother. She had never failed him. With his Lady's help he was ready to say "yes" to anything God would ask. Anything. . . .

6

Heaven—So Soon?

"Brother Jerome! Hurry...over here! Brother Maximilian's bleeding!"

The cry brought an abrupt halt to the soccer game. Jerome dashed across the field to where Maximilian was stretched out motionless on the grass.

"I'm . . . all right . . . really," Maximilian panted between coughs. "I just . . . felt . . . dizzy . . . for a minute."

"Don't try to move, Maximilian," Brother Jerome cautioned. "We'll get help." Jerome's face was grave as he turned to Brother Henry. "Call a driver to take him back to the house right away. It's serious enough. He's coughing up blood."

The doctor was summoned. His diagnosis came as a shock to everyone. Maximilian had tuberculosis.

Little by little, the pieces of the puzzle came together. Brother Maximilian had been sick for a long time. But because he had never complained or let others see that he didn't feel well, no one had ever dreamed just how serious his condition really was.

Father Cicchito, Maximilian's superior for two years, remembered that when Maximilian had first arrived from Poland his hands had always been cold. During the damp winter months, they would also break out in painful sores. But the doctors, even the specialists who were called in to examine him, had never suspected tuberculosis.

Brother Albert, one of Maximilian's classmates, later reported that Maximilian often suffered from severe headaches. Albert had discovered this by accident. He happened to notice that many times his friend's characteristic smile would suddenly and mysteriously turn into a wince of pain.

Maximilian's condition was serious, so serious, in fact, that it made him happy to think that the Lord might be calling him home to heaven. At the same time the idea that he was chosen to do something special for the spiritual good of people kept running through his mind. As always, Brother Maximilian turned to Mary. He prayed to her more than ever. God had a plan for him, and Mary would help him to carry it out. He would just have to be patient.

Being sick in bed, there wasn't much Maximilian could physically do to bring people closer to Jesus and Mary. But he could offer his sufferings for others. And he could pray. He did both.

"Look who's here!"
"Welcome back, Maximilian!"
"We've been really praying for you!"
"How are you feeling?"
It was the first time in two weeks that the young Franciscan had been allowed out of bed. Maximilian smiled broadly. It felt good to be back with his friends again.

After greeting each of the friars, Brother Maximilian called Brother Jerome and Father Joseph aside. He had something important to tell them. It couldn't wait any longer. As his two friends listened eagerly, Maximilian began to map out his plan.

"For a long time now, I've been thinking of how, with the help of our Blessed Mother, we could get together and do something practical to bring people back to God. This idea always comes to me when I'm praying, so I'm sure it must be from God." Brother Maximilian paused.

"Go on, Maximilian, go on. We're very interested in what you're saying," Father Joseph urged.

Brother Jerome nodded.

"I'm glad to hear that," Maximilian continued. "Of all our companions, I thought you would be the two who'd like to help start the new group. It will be like our Lady's own army! We'll do everything for her and with her, and our motto will be 'For the greatest glory of God.'" Maximilian concluded excitedly, "Since we'll be Mary's soldiers, and she is our Immaculate Mother, what do you think of calling the group 'The Knights of the Immaculata'?"

"That's a great name, Maximilian!" Jerome agreed enthusiastically, "When will we hold the first meeting?"

"I've also been thinking about that," replied Brother Maximilian. "Since we want to be sure that we're really doing God's will, we'll need to present the idea to our superior first. If Father Stephen approves, Jesus and Mary will be pleased by our obedience. I'll let you know the outcome as soon as I talk it over with Father. If he says yes, we'll schedule our first meeting in a few days."

7

A SOLDIER FOR HIS LADY

It was the evening of October 16, 1917. Seven shadows flitted in the candlelight. In a room at the Franciscan College in Rome, Brother Maximilian, Fathers Joseph, Quirico and Anthony, and Brothers Jerome, Anthony and Henry knelt in a semicircle. Before them, on a white-covered table, rested a small statue of the Immaculate Virgin flanked by two candles. All prayed for a few moments in silence. Then habits rustled and rosaries rattled as the friars took their seats. The meeting was underway.

"Tonight we can thank God and our Blessed Mother for the permission Father Stephen has given us to start our 'Knights of the Immaculata,'" Brother Maximilian joyfully announced. "Now there's no doubt that we're doing God's will."

"And how privileged we are to be the first members," Father Joseph added. "Did Father Stephen think it would be a good idea to invite others to join us?"

"Yes," Maximilian replied. "But he said we should go slowly because not all of our companions will understand the purpose of the Knights at first."

"You know, Maximilian," admitted Brother Quirico, "I'm not too sure that I understand just what we're supposed to be doing myself. I know that we want to help people to love God and the Blessed Mother, but how?"

Brother Maximilian smiled. "For now, Quirico, our main duty will be to pray and to spread devotion to our Lord and his Immaculate Mother by our special *tactics*. Later on, God will give us other powerful ways of drawing others closer to him."

"What do you mean by *tactics?*" asked Brother Henry, with a puzzled look on his face.

"Maybe he means that since we're Mary's army, we should use military terms to explain our work," suggested Brother Anthony.

"Yes!" Maximilian continued excitedly, "That's exactly it! And," he paused as he reached into the deep pocket of his habit, "these are the *shells* or *bullets* that we'll use to overcome our chief enemy, the devil. . . ."

The brothers watched in amazement as Maximilian drew out a handful of Miraculous Medals!

"Obedience will be one of our leading *weapons!*" exclaimed Brother Jerome.

"At the top of our list!" agreed Brother Maximilian.

"And love for God and his Mother will be our *defense*," Father Joseph added.

Everyone smiled and nodded.

After a few more minutes of discussion, the little group quietly made its way to the chapel. There Father Joseph blessed seven Miraculous Medals and put them on the first Knights of the Immaculata. Now the members were completely at Mary's service.

As Brother Maximilian walked back to his room, he felt strangely happy and fulfilled. *At last I'll be a soldier for my Lady,* he thought.

8

On Fire with Love

The beads of his rosary slipped slowly through Maximilian's fingers.

"Mother," he prayed as he came to the end of a decade, "Father Stephen was right. Not all of the friars understand what the Knights are all about. Not all of them accept us. I don't mind what others think or say about me, as long as your work can continue. I only ask you to help me to do God's will—no matter the cost."

Brother Maximilian had a lot to pray about. Certain members of his religious community wanted to put an end to the Knights of the Immaculata. Others just ignored the group. All of this hurt Maximilian, but it didn't stop him. He believed that everything that happened to him came from the hands of his mother, Mary. She hadn't failed him yet, and he knew she never would.

"What do you think about that Brother Maximilian?" one friar asked.

"What do you mean?" another replied.

"They say he's very intelligent and has a lot of good ideas. But lately he's been talking about using movies to spread the Gospel. I think that's going a bit too far. . . ."

Some said it was bad enough that Brother Maximilian had gotten together a group of followers, but now he was dreaming up impossible plans. Those who reasoned this way had overlooked an important fact, however, the fact that nothing is impossible with God. And Brother Maximilian never worked alone. He always did everything with the Lord and the Blessed Virgin.

Maximilian's plans did seem impractical back in 1917. He dreamt of using the movies, which had only been invented a few years earlier, to instruct people about God. He saw how crowds were flocking to the theaters, especially during the last days of World War I. People were desperately searching for relief from the terrible destruction and hopelessness of war. They wanted to run from reality and take shelter in an imaginary world where things were just as they had always been. Movies made this temporary escape possible. But some of the movies back then, just like some movies today, went against Gospel values. Instead of helping people to become better, they drew them farther and farther away from God. Brother Maximilian understood all this.

"Why can't we use the screen to teach goodness instead of evil?" he often asked his friends. "Just think of how we could spread the Word of God to millions through the movies!"

Brother Maximilian's plans didn't stop there. He was also thinking of printing and distributing good booklets and even a magazine to teach Jesus' Gospel to everyone. His burning desire was to lead all people to God.

9

A SECOND WONDER— AND THE CROSS

An aroma of freshly cut flowers mingled with the scent of wax from burning candles. Maximilian's heart was throbbing with excitement. It was that same feeling he had experienced so many years before on that unforgettable day when he had been visited by the Mother of God. Now, a second wonder was taking place. In a few minutes, he— Raymond Maximilian Kolbe—would become "another Christ."

The many years of prayer, study and hard work flashed through his memory as Brother Maximilian knelt before the bishop. Everything had led up to this sacred moment. Suddenly, Maximilian felt firm hands resting upon his head. He heard the bishop intone the prayer to the Holy Spirit. Maximilian's soul was now marked with a special sign. He was a priest forever.

No one could ever measure the great joy that filled the young priest's heart when he celebrated his first Mass the next morning. It was April 29, 1918. The flowers, the trees, the birds—all of nature which he loved so much—joined in the celebration, too. The Roman countryside was alive with color and beauty.

"This is my Body . . . This is my Blood. . . ." Father Maximilian's voice shook with emotion as he pronounced for the first time the words that changed the bread and wine into the Body and Blood of Jesus Christ!

How could he ever thank God enough for having chosen him to become a priest? After Mass, he knelt in prayer. *My Mother and my Queen, help me to thank the Lord for his great goodness to me. I am all yours, and everything I have I give to you. Do with me whatever will please God the most.*

The July sun made his room stifling. On top of that, Maximilian, propped up on two pillows, his rosary in his hand, was burning with fever. Upon his return to Poland a year after his ordination, he had suffered a serious relapse of the nagging tuberculosis. The doctors had already removed a portion of his lungs. He was so sick now that they gave

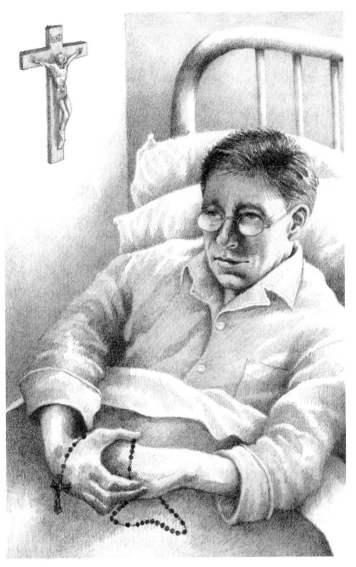

He had suffered a serious relapse of tuberculosis.

him only three months to live. But Father Maximilian hadn't become sad or discouraged. He had only doubled his prayers.

Whenever he was permitted to get up, the determined priest set to work planning for the foundation of Mary's Knights there at the Cracow monastery.

By August of that same year, 1920, Father Maximilian had become so weak that his superiors decided to admit him to the tuberculosis sanatorium at Zakopane. Eight months later he was moved to another sanatorium in the town of Nieszaw.

Finally . . . "Father, I have good news for you." The doctor smiled kindly as he leaned over the bed. "I spoke with your superior this morning. . . ."

"You did?" Father Maximilian eagerly sat up.

"Yes. Both he and I agreed that since you're feeling stronger, we'll allow you to go home to Cracow. But remember now, you're not cured. You still have to take things easy and . . ."

"Leave everything in God's hands!" Maximilian cheerfully interrupted. "Yes, Doctor, I'm sure he'll take good care of me.

Thank you for all your help. Let's not forget to pray for each other."

The doctor gave a firm squeeze to his patient's outstretched hand and turned quickly away. He didn't want the priest to see his tears of admiration. But Father Maximilian wouldn't have noticed. He was already out of bed busily gathering his few belongings. After over a year spent recuperating in the hospital, he was anxious to go home.

10

MARY'S MAGAZINE

Back in Cracow, Father Maximilian set to work again. More and more young men came to join him. They wanted to dedicate their lives to God as friars in the Franciscan Order. They wanted to spread knowledge of Jesus and Mary in the quickest and most effective ways possible.

Early in 1922, Maximilian and his friars began publishing a small magazine dedicated to the Blessed Mother. They had no money, no experience and no printing press of their own. But they did have strong faith in God. And that was more than enough. The friars called their new magazine *The Knight of the Immaculata.* The first issue wasn't very attractive. It was even printed without a cover! In spite of its poor quality, people soon began to subscribe.

Well, Maximilian, you'll just have to find some way to pay the printer. When I gave you

permission to begin the magazine, it was only on the condition that you cover the expenses. The superior's words echoed in his memory as Father Maximilian vested for Mass. "Mary," he prayed, "you've taken care of everything else so far. Now please take care of our bills."

The Blessed Mother didn't disappoint him. After Mass, Maximilian noticed an envelope lying beside Mary's statue. He walked over and picked it up. Opening it, he found the exact sum of money that he owed the printer!

Although his superiors allowed him to continue to print the magazine, other priests and brothers complained and criticized. "Saint Francis never meant us to be printers," they grumbled. "We're supposed to be preaching and hearing confessions."

Father Maximilian could have argued that he *was* preaching through his magazine—and to more people than might ever come to church—but he kept silent. The others would understand, someday.

Maximilian waited a while before going back to his provincial superior with another request. "Father, we need to buy our own printing press," he explained. "In one year we've had to change printers five times. It's very hard to work like this."

The superior patiently shook his head. "I give you permission, Maximilian, as long as you find the money to pay for it."

As usual, Maximilian had no idea where the money would come from. But once again the Lord stepped in. Just around this time, Father Lawrence Cyman, an American Franciscan priest, came to visit Maximilian's community. At recreation one night, some of the friars ridiculed Father Maximilian and his magazine. Now, they reported, he even had the wild idea of buying a printing press. Maximilian lowered his head and said nothing. Father Lawrence listened. When it was quiet again, he spoke. "Instead of just making fun of Father Maximilian, wouldn't it be better to help him?" An embarrassed silence followed. It was broken by the American priest. He turned to face Maximilian and said, "I'd like to make an offering to help your work, Father. I'll send you something when I return to the United States."

True to his word, Father Lawrence later sent Father Maximilian a check for $100.00 —a small fortune in those days.

"He can't bring a printing press into our Cracow monastery!" one of the priests exclaimed in exasperation. "We just don't have the room."

"You're right, Father," answered the provincial superior. "Not only that, but it would disrupt the community schedule. I think it would be best to send Father Maximilian to Grodno. The monastery there needs repair, but at least it's spacious. He can open a print shop on the grounds."

And so Father Maximilian moved to Grodno, a town at the opposite end of Poland.

No one could have imagined what was yet to come.

11

SHARING THE MASTER'S WEALTH

"Let's try tightening this," suggested Father Maximilian to Brother Albert, giving a bolt a few quick turns. With an explosion of booms and bangs, the second-hand printing press suddenly rattled to life. The two "mechanics" sighed in relief. Taking a step backward, they admired the machine that from then on would print only for God.

"How good the Lord was to arrange the visit of that American priest," Brother Albert thought aloud. "Without his help we'd never have been able to pay for this press."

"Yes," Maximilian agreed, "Father Lawrence really understands our work." With a knowing smile he added, "Don't worry, Albert. Someday many more will understand it, too."

Someone else already understood, as did Father Maximilian, the great power of the communications media and its potential good. He was a holy Italian priest named Father James Alberione. Father Alberione was also using the printing press to preach the Gospel of Jesus and to instruct people about God. He had begun his work in 1915, seven years before Father Maximilian. Father Alberione even founded two new religious congregations to continue this important work: the Society of St. Paul, for men, and the Daughters of St. Paul, for women. Today these priests, brothers and sisters also use movies, radio, television, music, DVDs, apps, e-books, and the Internet to bring God's word to the greatest number of people possible. Father Maximilian and Father Alberione shared many ideas and goals in common, although they didn't know one another.

At Grodno, Father Maximilian and the friars worked harder than ever. They stayed up late at night printing Mary's magazine. Sometimes their fingertips bled because of their long hours at the machines. Although they often didn't have enough to eat, they used the tiny income they received from the magazine to purchase more tools and better machines for the service of God.

The members of Mary's Knights tried always to walk in the footsteps of their patron, Saint Francis of Assisi. Like Saint

Francis they loved to be poor. This made them more similar to Jesus. . . .

"Brother Zeno, I'll be needing my shoes today for the trip to Warsaw."

"Of course, Father Maximilian. I have them right here."

"Thank you, Zeno. I'll return them as soon as I get home."

Incredibly, the friars were so poor that those who wore the same size even shared their shoes and clothing! Yet, they were always happy because they did everything out of love. And love makes even hard things easy. In a real sense, the friars were wealthy. They were rich in faith and in love of God. Being full of this love, they wanted to share it with others by printing and distributing good magazines and booklets about God and the Blessed Virgin. The Knights of the Immaculata were carrying out the advice Jesus gave the very first apostles: "The gift you have received, give as a gift" (Matthew 10:8).

12

TRAPPED!

The number of subscribers to *The Knight of the Immaculata* continued to soar. Soon the friars were able to obtain bigger and better printing presses. The search was then begun for a special motor to generate power to run the machines.

Father Maximilian learned that Mr. Borowski, a gentleman in town, owned a diesel motor. He decided to pay him a visit. All the way out to Mr. Borowski's house, Maximilian prayed one Hail Mary after another that the owner would be inspired to sell his precious piece of equipment. As always, the Blessed Mother rewarded Maximilian's trust. Not only did Mr. Borowski agree to sell his motor, but he also accompanied the priest back to the monastery in order to personally install it.

As he worked, the good-natured man shyly confessed to one of the friars that he had been away from the Church and the sacraments for twenty years. Of course, Father Maximilian soon learned about this sad situation. He and all the friars began storming heaven for the conversion of their friend.

One day, they finally succeeded in coaxing Mr. Borowski to pay a quick visit to their chapel.

"All right, all right. A visit maybe, but no confession, eh? Remember that!" their benefactor reminded with a wave of his hand.

"Don't worry about anything. Nobody will even see you," a young brother promised, ushering the older man over to a small kneeler with a screen fixed to its top.

"This is the strangest kind of pew I've ever seen," Mr. Borowski muttered to himself. He knelt down. A few minutes passed. He tried to pray, but it had been so long .. . . Suddenly, out of the corner of his eye, he saw Father Maximilian approaching. To his astonishment, he noticed that Father was wearing the purple stole worn during the sacrament of Penance. Before the bewildered man had time to react, the priest had taken a seat on the opposite side of the screen. "And now, my son, how long has it been since your last confession?" he asked kindly.

Mr. Borowski was caught in a holy trap. Tears rolled unashamedly down his face as he opened up his soul to Father Maximilian, whom he knew took the very place of Jesus.

From that day on, Mr. Borowski came often to visit his Lord in the Holy Eucharist. Never again would he stay away from Mass or the sacraments.

Father Maximilian gave all the credit for this happy change to the Blessed Mother. With a twinkle in his eye, he loved to repeat, "Brothers, remember that our Lady always rewards even the smallest favor that we do for her. The case of Mr. Borowski proves this. He came here simply to install a machine so that Mary's work could go ahead. And look at how she led him back to Jesus! How powerful and kind our Immaculate Mother is!"

13

A Statue and a Conquest

The battered little alarm clock announced a new day. Father Maximilian struggled out of bed. He got slowly to his knees before his statue of the Blessed Virgin. He felt so weak. But he was never too sick to pray. "My Lady," he whispered, "please increase my faith. I know that I'm back in the hospital only because God has permitted it. I want to do his will, never my own."

The Lord permitted Maximilian to stay in the hospital for six long months of the year 1926. During that time the young priest suffered not only in his body but in his mind and spirit as well. He felt as if he were good for nothing. He believed that he was a burden to his brothers because he was always getting sick. He was discouraged because he couldn't work as hard as he wanted to. But his worst suffering was the thought that God and the Blessed Mother had abandoned him. It wasn't true, of course. The thought was a temptation. The devil was trying with all his might to prevent Father Maximilian from continuing his good work.

Maximilian prayed. It didn't matter that he no longer felt the presence of Jesus and Mary. He believed that they still loved him and were very close to him.

In the end, the frail priest came through this trial of spirit with stronger faith than ever. Little by little, to the astonishment of all the doctors, his health began to improve. The only person who wasn't surprised was Maximilian himself. After all, weren't God and the Blessed Mother more powerful than all the doctors' prescriptions put together? They could certainly arrange for his release from the hospital. And they did!

Father Maximilian had hardly set foot back at Grodno, when all the friars clustered around him shouting excitedly, "Father, have you heard? Have you heard?"

"One at a time, please. Have I heard what?" the priest asked in amusement.

"About our magazine!" Brother Anthony practically shouted, making a genuine effort to stay calm. "We've just calculated that our total circulation for this year was 45,000 copies. In 1924, it was only 12,000. This means that the circulation has more than tripled in just two years, Father!"

Father Maximilian's thin face beamed with joy. He was delighted, not only with the growth of Mary's little magazine, but also with the zeal and generosity of his good friars. The priest's steady gaze scanned the circle of nineteen young faces. He made a decision. He knew it was time to ask his superiors about moving the monastery and the magazine to larger quarters.

Permission was granted, and the friars began looking for a suitable place. The very next summer they heard that there was a beautiful plot of land for sale in Teresin, just outside the city of Warsaw. A few of the brothers went with Father Maximilian to inspect the property. They all agreed that it was just what they had been looking for. Maximilian inquired about the price. It was very high. "How could we ever afford it?" several of the brothers asked.

"Don't worry," Father Maximilian reassured. "If it's God's will that we move here, Mary herself will take care of everything."

The priest then went ahead and placed a statue of the Blessed Virgin right in the middle of the empty lot.

Because of his vows of poverty and obedience, Father Maximilian couldn't buy the property without the permission of his provincial superior. He asked for the necessary permission, but soon the provincial replied that the land was too expensive.

Maximilian didn't discuss the matter any further. He was sure that in obeying his superior he was obeying God himself. The only thing left to do was to notify the property owner, a nobleman named Prince Lubecki, that he wouldn't be purchasing the land after all.

The next day found Father Maximilian knocking at the great door of Prince Lubecki's mansion. A butler answered. He promptly escorted the priest into an elegantly furnished parlor. When the prince finally stepped in, Father Maximilian was completely absorbed in praying his rosary.

"Good afternoon, Father. You've come with your superior's answer, I presume."

"I am sorry, sir, I didn't hear you," Father Maximilian apologized, jumping to his feet. "I won't take up much of your time. I've just come to tell you that we're unable to purchase the land."

Prince Lubecki was surprised at this news. Yet, when he saw how humble and kind Father Maximilian was, he decided to donate the property, as long as the Franciscans would promise to celebrate Masses for his intentions.

Sometimes strange things happen in life—strange to us, but all a part of God's mysterious plan. One of these took place then. When Maximilian's superiors heard that the prince would give them the property if they would celebrate Masses for him, they refused the arrangement, saying that they wanted the land "with no strings attached."

Once again, Father Maximilian called on the prince. This time he had to explain that his superiors wanted the property without any conditions.

Although Prince Lubecki was very impressed by Father Maximilian's humility and sincerity, he was quite disturbed at the news. "If this is how things stand, take away that statue you've set up!" he demanded.

But Maximilian didn't. He informed the nobleman that he would return in three days, then quietly left.

The prince had much to do, but he was so upset about the whole matter that he couldn't concentrate. Finally he could stand it no longer. *I'll give them that land anyway,* he thought. As soon he came to this decision, he felt calm and even happy again.

After three days Father Maximilian returned as he had promised. "Take your statue!" the prince exclaimed. "And take the land it stands on. It's yours!"

The Blessed Virgin had won again.

Mary's Knights now had all the room they needed to expand. Soon Father Maximilian's dream—The City of the Immaculata (*Niepokalanow* in Polish)—would be a reality.

14

NIEPOKALANOW

"Have more to eat. Don't be shy," Father Maximilian encouraged. "Remember, this is your home now. You're part of the family."

"Thank you, Father," the teenager managed to murmur between bites of home-made rye bread.

Everything I've heard about Father Maximilian is really true, he thought. *He reminds me very much of both my own parents, so kind and yet so strong.*

Father Maximilian's sudden move to pour Jan a refill of milk called the boy's thoughts back to the present. "Father," he impulsively exclaimed, "you don't know how happy I am to be here!"

"Good, good," the priest approved, with a reflective stroke of his beard. "And you'll always be happy if you give yourself entirely to Jesus and Mary." Then, sensing that the boy was still a bit homesick, Father Maximilian confided, "You know, Jan, this morning during Mass I thanked Jesus and our Immaculate Mother for sending you here to join us."

"You did?" The boy's blue eyes widened in surprise.

"Yes, I did," Maximilian went on. "And I asked them to send many other generous young men like you to carry on their work."

Jan was beginning to feel more and more at ease. "How many friars live and work here at Niepokalanow, Father?"

"Well, when we first began several years ago, there were twenty of us," the priest replied. "But we've grown since then. Why don't we go on a little tour now so you can see for yourself?" he added with a grin.

The "little tour" lasted until it was time to go to bed. There was just so much to see. Besides the gigantic rotary presses which by then (1939) were rolling out one million copies of Mary's magazine a month, Niepokalanow was equipped with its own lumber mill, fire department, and radio station. As for the community, there were over 500 Franciscans, most of them brothers, doing everything from cooking and farming to writing, editing and printing!

Jan could hardly believe what he saw. As they left one cluster of buildings and headed

*Gigantic presses rolled out a million copies
of Mary's magazine each month.*

for the next, he gave a shy tug to Father Maximilian's wide sleeve.

"Father, why is everyone so quiet as they work? Aren't you allowed to talk here?"

Father Maximilian chuckled. "Let's go visit Jesus and then I'll explain everything."

The priest led the way to another simple building. "This is our chapel, Jan," he reverently announced.

A silent push of the door revealed rows and rows of brothers kneeling in motionless adoration before their Eucharistic Master. They were praying not only for themselves, but for the people who would read their magazine and booklets.

The boy was impressed. "They all look so holy," he whispered.

"They're all working to become saints, Jan. That's why they came here," Father whispered back. After a few moments of prayer, Father Maximilian arose and made a beautiful genuflection. Jan imitated him.

Out in the courtyard again, the priest turned to the boy. "Well, have you discovered our secret yet? I'll give you a hint: it has to do both with chapel and with our work."

Jan was eager to confirm his guess. "I think I do know the secret behind Niepokalanow, Father Maximilian. It's prayer! I understand now why the friars keep silent as they work," the young man excitedly continued. "It's because they're talking with God. While they run their machines or plow the fields the friars are continuing the conversations they began with Jesus in the chapel."

"Yes, Jan," Father Maximilian approved. "You've discovered the whole secret of our success. Before we do anything here in Mary's City, we pray. What good could we do by ourselves? It's only with God's help that we're able to accomplish things. We do everything for Jesus and Mary. And from them alone we expect our reward."

Just then the bell signaling the end of the workday began echoing its call to prayer. Almost immediately, friars began appearing from every corner, making their way to chapel. As Father Maximilian and his newest spiritual son mingled in with a passing group, the boy quietly repeated, "I'm so happy to be here!"

15

THE LESSON OF THE VS

The years sped by. Life in Niepokalanow, the City of the Immaculata, went ahead with joy and zeal. Soon Mary had *two* of her own small cities. . . .

One of Father Maximilian's greatest dreams was to print magazines and booklets about Jesus and Mary not only in his own Polish language, but also in all languages. And so, in 1930, he left the community at Niepokalanow and the publishing of *The Knight of the Immaculata* under the capable leadership of his younger brother, Joseph— Father Alphonse—and set out with four brothers for the Far East.

They stopped first in Shanghai, China, where two of the brothers remained to find members for the Knights of the Immaculata. The other two brothers traveled on with Father Maximilian to Japan. There, in the city of Nagasaki, they set up a little City of the Immaculata, just like the one back in Poland. In Japanese it was called *Mugenzai No Sono*.

It wasn't easy for the Polish Franciscans to get used to the complicated Japanese language with its 2,000 different characters. But, with much prayer and effort, they succeeded. And soon they were printing *The Knight of the Immaculata* in Japanese.

Meanwhile, sad news arrived from Poland. Young Father Alphonse, such a dedicated and faithful follower of his older brother, had died of pneumonia during the novena in preparation for the feast of the Immaculate Conception.

Perhaps God had given some forewarning to Father Maximilian about his brother's death. It's said that before leaving for the Far East, Maximilian had gone to say good-bye to Alphonse, whom he had found sleeping. Instead of waking his brother, Father Maximilian had just kissed him on the forehead, saying, "Sleep on, my brother. No other rest in the service of the Immaculata is better earned. Farewell. . . . Who knows whether we will see one another on earth again!"

At Father Alphonse's funeral, a journalist praised the work of the youngest Kolbe brother: "Here he is, a poor friar whose editing office was a bare and simple room. Clothed in a Franciscan habit, faded and patched, he persevered in work and prayer directed to the great Mother of God. . . . He taught crowds of young people about God."

The death of Father Alphonse left a great emptiness at Niepokalanow. In faraway Japan, Father Maximilian also felt his brother's death greatly. From there he wrote to his mother, "I used white vestments in celebrating Mass for Father Alphonse, because today was the feast of the Immaculate Conception. Certainly he is already in heaven. Mary Immaculate took him to herself during the novena of her feast day. One can only envy him. He lived, suffered, worked and sacrificed himself for Mary. She called him to herself during her novena. We, too, will follow him, because we live only in order to reach heaven."

After five years in the East, with only one brief visit to Poland, Father Maximilian became very ill again and had to return to his native country. But his thoughts still reached out to the whole world. "Someday we must go to India to teach the people there about Jesus," Maximilian urged his friars.

"We should also begin printing Mary's magazine in Arabic, Turkish, Persian and Hebrew! We must preach the Gospel to the ends of the earth!"

Following Maximilian's return to Niepokalanow, the city buzzed with new progress. The friars began putting out their own newspaper (several editions a day), while the number of readers continued to multiply. Besides *The Knight of the Immaculata*, two new magazines were begun, one for children and one for teenagers. But always, amid the roar of the printing presses or in the stillness of their chapel, the friars prayed. After all, their most important work was to become saints. Father Maximilian had impressed this fact on them in a way that none would ever forget.

"v = V" was all the blackboard read. All eyes were fixed on Maximilian as he began the explanation of the strange equation. "It's very simple, Brothers. The small v stands for my will, and the large V is the will of God. If my will goes against the will of God, the two Vs intersect—like this." He turned and drew a large cross on the board. "This is how many small crosses come into our lives," he explained. "Instead, if we try hard always to do God's will by obeying him, the two Vs will never cross."

A sigh came from the back of the room. "Father, you make it sound so easy to become a saint," a young brother meekly protested.

"Oh, but it is, Brother, it is!" Father Maximilian quickly assured him. "Keep in mind that God wants us all to be good and holy. All we have to do is cooperate and obey him. And remember this for as long as you live...." The urgency in the priest's voice and the fire in his dark eyes grew stronger. "There is no good action, no matter how difficult or even heroic it might be, that we can't perform with the aid of our Immaculate Mother!"

Little did the friars know how often they would need to remember this truth in the days ahead.

16

EXILE

"Sound the siren! Everyone down to the bomb shelters. And pray Brothers! Pray!"

Robed figures immediately appeared, darting frantically through piles of burning rubble. Father Maximilian remained calm and courageous as the ground beneath him trembled and the sky blazed angrily with fire and debris. It was September 1, 1939. Poland was being invaded by Germany. The little country was caught in the terrible grip of World War II.

Day after day and night after night, bombs fell like deadly raindrops on large cities and tiny villages. Nothing and no one was spared. Not even Niepokalanow.

Every tense and fearful expression relaxed into a smile of relief as Father Maximilian climbed into the shelter. The friars looked expectantly at him. Maximilian motioned for silence. "Brothers, what I have to tell you now hurts me as much as it's going to hurt you."

An invisible wave of dread swept through the underground room. Father Maximilian could no longer hide his sorrow. "After much prayer, I've come to an important decision. The time has come to carry out the instructions that our provincial superior has given for such an emergency. All of you must leave Niepokalanow and seek shelter—in our other monasteries or with your families. You won't be safe here. . . ." the priest's voice broke as he read signs of shock and pain on each upturned face. "God willing, when all this is over, we'll return home once again to Niepokalanow," he managed to finish.

There was complete silence. A few seconds, which seemed more like hours, passed. Then one by one came the pathetic pleas.

"Father, let me stay with you. Please, for the love of our Lady. I'll die here with you if I have to. . . ."

"And I, I'm strong. I'm not afraid, Father Maximilian. You'll need help to take care of the injured. You know I've always been good at first aid. . . ."

"Don't forget me, Father Maximilian. I don't want to leave either. Remember many years ago when I first came here? You told me that Niepokalanow was my home. It is my home, and always will be. Please don't send me away now. . . ."

Father Maximilian fought back hot, stinging tears. He allowed a courageous group of friars who had begged to stay—five priests and about fifty brothers—to remain at Niepokalanow. The others were all to leave.

A sorrowful line began to form. Each friar in turn knelt to receive his father's farewell blessing. In a few short hours, the entire population of Mary's City dwindled to nearly a tenth of what it had been.

Days dragged by. As the war increased in fury the friars multiplied their prayers, work and sacrifices. Maximilian tried to keep everyone's spirits up with his optimism and his example of trust in Jesus and Mary. Deep in his heart he couldn't help feeling that this was only the beginning—the beginning of a new and mysterious mission for Mary's Knights.

17

ON MISSION TO CALVARY

"Watch over your sons, Mary. Bless them with a quiet and restful night." Maximilian noiselessly closed the dormitory door behind him. All the friars were safe and sound. Now he too could steal a few hours of sleep.

Maximilian had no way of knowing that this would be the last peaceful night he or any of the friars would have for a long, long time.

The rooster's crow signaled the dawn of September 19, 1939. Mary's City woke from sleep. The small band of priests and brothers gathered in the chapel for meditation and Mass as they had always done. Then came breakfast. And . . .

"Father! Father Maximilian! German motorcycles are heading toward the main gate!"

All eyes in the refectory turned to Maximilian. They all knew what this meant. The priest's hands reached instinctively for the rosary at his side.

"Let's go to meet them," he quietly answered.

The Nazi soldiers were quick about their cruel business. "You're all under arrest!" bellowed the leader, as the soldiers began marching the friars out to their waiting trucks.

"Two of you can stay behind to take care of the wounded," the commander said to Father Maximilian in a lower tone.

"I'll come with you," the priest replied calmly, "two of the brothers will tend the injured."

After two days of traveling, part of the way on foot and the rest in overcrowded trucks and animal wagons, the friars reached Amtitz in Germany. Amtitz was one of the smaller concentration camps, but a terrible place nonetheless. The prisoners were given very little to eat. The barracks were damp. The filth was incredible. Yet even in the midst of this suffering, Father Maximilian remained smiling and peaceful. After all, the Blessed Mother was with them. What did they have to fear?

At least the German soldiers gave the friars some freedom, and Maximilian was able to comfort and encourage his followers. "Do you remember how I once told you that there's nothing we can't do without our Blessed Mother's help?" he questioned one evening as the friars trudged back to camp after a scorching day's work in the fields.

"Yes, Father," came the unanimous reply.

"Well, now is the time to put this trust into real practice." Father Maximilian's eyes shone with happiness. "Never forget, Brothers, we're members of Mary's Knights. The Blessed Mother has sent us here on a special mission. . . ."

"Tell us what this mission is," Brother Joseph pleaded.

"Yes, Father, please explain it to us," the others begged.

"I'll be happy to," Maximilian replied. "Our mission is this: Mary wishes us to pray and offer up all our sacrifices so that many souls will go to heaven. She wants us to walk with Jesus to Calvary. Let's do our best now to make this important assignment a success!"

Father Maximilian was determined not to disappoint his Lady. Even though he was so sickly, he labored as hard as anyone else in the prison camp. A single day's work left him weak and completely exhausted. Yet, night after night, while the others slept, the holy priest prayed. How many times a glimpse of his kneeling shadow comforted the frightened brothers who awoke in the middle of the night.

Maximilian's prayers were heard. His heavenly Mother repaid his trust with a special gift. On December 8, 1939, the feast of her Immaculate Conception, he and all of the friars were released from the camp and allowed to return to Niepokalanow.

18

"I Believe!"

"It will take quite a bit of work, Father, but we think we can repair the damage done by the bombs and the vandals," Brother Andrew reported.

"And the print shop can still be salvaged," Brother Jan joined in.

"We can be sure that it was Jesus and Mary who saved Niepokalanow," Father Maximilian commented softly as the three continued their inspection. "All praise and thanksgiving to them."

Little by little, many of the exiled friars came home to Mary's City. There were some, however, who couldn't return. These were the friars who had helped Father Maximilian to write and edit Mary's magazine and other religious booklets. Now they were being hunted by the Nazi police. If caught, they would be punished for the "crime" of having taught people about God!

Father Maximilian knew that soon enough these same police would come back for him. The Nazi invaders planned to do away with all of Poland's leaders, especially the religious ones. The Nazis realized that once these persons were out of the way, the rest of the people could be easily conquered.

Maximilian prepared himself with prayer for whatever was coming. The friars, too, prayed more than ever before. They kept watch day and night before the Blessed Sacrament. They begged God for the strength to continue printing and spreading religious truths in the face of so much danger.

A year passed. Then on February 17, 1941, it happened. Two black cars, marked with the symbol of the Nazi police, pulled up in front of Niepokalanow. Five Nazis jumped out. The brother at the door hastily telephoned Father Maximilian. He came to greet the Germans.

After a few preliminary questions, the Nazis began a thorough search of the monastery. Finally, motioning to Father Maximilian and the four other priests they had rounded up, the German soldiers ordered, "Get into the cars!" All five priests obeyed. The doors slammed shut. The cars sped away. Father Maximilian knew that he would never see Niepokalanow again.

The priests were brought to Pawiak, a horrible prison in the city of Warsaw.

Immediately, Maximilian set to work. He administered the sacrament of Penance to his fellow prisoners. He comforted them. He prayed with them.

Some time after his arrival, Father Maximilian was transferred to Cell 103. He and his fellow inmates were subjected to a "prisoner inspection."

"What's this?" the Nazi officer growled when he came to Maximilian, still wearing his Franciscan habit. Violently grabbing the crucifix of the rosary hanging at Father Maximilian's side, he waved it before the priest's face.

"Fool! Do you believe in this thing?"

"Yes, I believe!" came the calm reply.

The outraged officer dealt Maximilian a vicious blow in the face.

"Do you still believe?" the Nazi screamed.

"Yes, with all my heart!"

A stronger punch followed.

The officer's face was purple with fury. "And what about now?" he screeched.

"Yes, yes, I believe!"

The defeated Nazi slammed his brutal fist into Maximilian's face a third time before stomping out of the cell.

"Don't worry; don't be upset," Father Maximilian told his shaken fellow prisoners.

"You have serious problems of your own. This is a small thing for me to offer up to Jesus and Mary."

19

In Mary's Hands

The friars back at Niepokalanow tried every way possible to have Father Maximilian released. Twenty of them even went to the Nazis and offered to take his place in the prison. But the answer was "No." The Nazis well knew that the minute they released him he would go on writing about God and the Blessed Mother. And that was the last thing they wanted.

Soon word came that Maximilian was being transferred to Auschwitz. It was the worst of the concentration camps, a place once described as the closest thing possible to hell on earth.

"Run, foolish priest! And no more falling, or you know what you'll get!" snarled the commanding officer.

Father Maximilian could go on no longer. The heavy load of wood piled high on his back was too much for him. He slumped to the ground. Immediately came the wild lashes of the whip. Maximilian staggered to his feet. In a few seconds he lay sprawled on the ground again. And so it went hour after hour, day after day.

To any of his fellow prisoners who asked him how he could accept these tortures so calmly, the priest would answer with a smile, "Our Blessed Mother is helping me to suffer all of this for her Son."

Every night the prisoners took turns creeping to Maximilian's side. They knew he would be by his bunk, hearing confessions. It didn't matter to him that he would be harshly punished if he were caught. The only thing he was concerned about was the spiritual good of others.

Father Maximilian also had the habit of giving away his food, even when he received only half the regular portion because he was too weak to do the required work.

The priest was always cheerful. He tried to spread joy in the midst of so much sorrow and suffering. He was constantly repeating to his fellow prisoners, "Call on Mary. Put yourself in her hands. She will keep you close to Jesus. She will never fail you. Never."

As July came to a close, a frightening thing happened in Maximilian's cellblock—Block 14. The roll call revealed that someone had escaped. The rest of the prisoners stood frozen in horror at the news. They knew the punishment. Ten men from their group would now be sentenced to die—by starvation.

"All prisoners will remain standing until further notice!" the commandant howled.

The late afternoon heat was overpowering. Some prisoners began to faint. Father Maximilian continued to stand motionless and serene. He was deep in prayer.

20

BOTH CROWNS AT LAST

The next morning, the fugitive had still not been found. After the roll call, all the inmates except those of Block 14 were sent to their work assignments.

"Block 14, line up!" shouted a Nazi officer. "You will stand here—all day. And remember, no water for any of them," he barked at the wardens assigned to keep watch.

Hours passed. Weak from heavy work and lack of food, many of the prisoners began to faint and drop to the ground. They were left there to die. Father Maximilian remained standing.

At about 3:00 pm, the Block 14 prisoners were allowed a half-hour for the delayed noon meal. After that, they were again forced to line up and stand in the scorching heat.

The sun was beginning its slow downward climb. Night roll call had just ended when Commandant Fritsch appeared on the scene wearing a frightening look of triumph. The surviving prisoners stood in suspense, waiting to hear the names of those destined for starvation. Up and down the rows of trembling prisoners Fritsch swaggered, picking out the ten who would die.

"You! . . . and you there! . . . And the one behind him, too. . . ."

A heartrending sob escaped from one of the "chosen" men. "No! Please!" cried Francis Gajowniczek. "What will happen to my wife and children?"

Suddenly, Father Maximilian stepped out of line. He stood at attention before Fritsch.

"What do you want?" the commandant growled.

Pointing toward Gajowniczek, in a steady voice Maximilian replied, "I'm a Polish Catholic priest. I want to take his place because he has a wife and children."

Fritsch couldn't believe what was happening. For a long moment he said nothing. What could he say in the face of such heroism? Finally, he cleared his throat. He tried to sound gruff and threatening, but somehow his voice had lost much of its force. "I accept," he said shortly. Then, gesturing to Gajowniczek who was still standing with

"I want to take his place."

the condemned men, he ordered, "Out!" The stunned prisoner returned to the ranks. And Father Maximilian stepped into line behind those sentenced to die. "Come with us, Mother," he prayed. "We'll need you now more than ever."

Down into the windowless starvation cell the condemned men filed. All their clothes were taken from them. The only door out was securely bolted. Everything was set for the torture to begin. But then something happened which completely bewildered the Nazi soldiers. Softly at first, and then louder and louder, singing began to rise from the underground dungeon.

"I always knew that priest was crazy," one officer scoffed. "And his band of fools imitates everything he does—even now."

"Shut up and listen!" his companion retorted. "They're singing hymns—the kind I sang in church as a boy. . . ."

It was true. Father Maximilian and his "parishioners" were singing. And soon enough they had other prisoners in nearby cells praying and singing with them. We don't know of any of the conversations that took place in that pitch-black cave. But we do have the eyewitness reports of Bruno Borgowiec. Mr. Borgowiec, a Polish prisoner who was fluent in German, was sent down into the starvation bunker each day to translate for the Nazi guards and to record the names of those who prisoners who had died. "Every day the rosary and other prayers and religious hymns echoed through the whole subterranean area," he later wrote. "It seemed to me that I was in church. Father Maximilian started and all the men responded. . . . Toward the end, when they were all very weak, they whispered their prayers. Every time the cell door was opened, there was Father Maximilian—sometimes kneeling, sometimes standing in the midst of the men and looking very peaceful."

The agonizing days stretched into one week, two weeks, then a third. Mary would soon be coming to take her son to heaven.

On August 14, 1941, the day before the feast of Mary's Assumption into heaven, four prisoners were left in the starvation cell. Only Father Maximilian was still alert. His three companions had all lost consciousness and were close to death. The priest had prepared them to meet their Creator. In a few short minutes, he, too, would be seeing God. Father was too weak to kneel. But that didn't matter. What counted was that he was still able to pray.

"Holy Mary, Mother of God, pray for us sinners, now. . . ." The door banged open. ". . .and at the hour of our death. Amen." A Nazi soldier came toward him with a deadly hypodermic needle. Father Maximilian understood. The Nazis were coming to speed up his passage to heaven! He smiled as he offered the soldier his pitifully thin arm. Soon he would be with Jesus and Mary. He felt his Immaculate Mother's presence there. She had personally come to bring him the white crown of purity and the red crown of martyrdom that he had chosen so long ago. At last they would be his. At last.

Father Maximilian Kolbe was beatified by Pope Paul VI in 1971 and proclaimed a saint by Pope John Paul II on October 10, 1982. We celebrate his feast day each year on August 14.

PRAYER

Saint Maximilian, thank you for your powerful example of love. You loved the Lord and his Mother Mary with all your heart. Your love made you discover new ways to bring people closer to God. It kept you peaceful and hopeful during the terrible sufferings of the concentration camp. It even gave you the courage to lay down your life for a man you didn't know.

I have many chances every day to show my love for God and my neighbor. But sometimes it's hard to love.

Saint Maximilian, I know that you understand. Remind me that Mary is always eager to help me and lead me closer to Jesus. With Jesus and Mary I want to live and love as you did. Please pray for me. Amen.

Glossary

1. **Assumption, Feast of the**—the day (August 15) on which the Church celebrates the privilege God gave Mary in taking her body and soul into heaven at the end of her earthly life.

2. **Beatify**—the act by which the Pope, in the name of the Catholic Church, declares that a deceased person lived a life of Gospel holiness in a heroic way. This is done after the person's life and holiness have been carefully researched. A proven miracle resulting from the holy person's prayers to God on behalf of someone else is also needed for beatification. A person who has been beatified is called by the title "Blessed." Beatification is the second step in the process of naming someone a saint.

3. **Blessed Sacrament**—another name for the Holy Eucharist, the real Body and Blood of the risen Jesus present under the appearance of bread and wine at Mass. The name Blessed Sacrament is especially used to refer to the Holy Eucharist kept in the form of consecrated Hosts in the tabernacle.

4. **Canonize**—the act by which the Pope declares that a deceased person has lived Christian virtues to a heroic degree, is now in heaven, and may be honored by the whole Church. Canonization is the name given to the ceremony in which a person is given the title "Saint." Canonization comes after beatification. It requires a second miracle credited to the holy person's intercession before God.

5. **Eucharistic Benediction**—the ceremony in which a priest or a deacon blesses the people with the consecrated Host enclosed in a special vessel (container) called a monstrance. The monstrance has a round window through which the people can see the sacred Host.

6. **Friar**—a word meaning "brother." It is the name given to male members (both priests and brothers) of certain religious orders, such as the Franciscans and Dominicans. While a monk usually works and prays inside his monastery, a friar usually ministers to God's people outside the monastery.

7. **Habit**—distinctive clothing worn by members of a religious order.

8. **Immaculata**—a title given to Mary, the Mother of God. It especially honors her Immaculate Conception, the privilege God gave Mary in preserving her from sin from the very beginning of her existence. God kept Mary free from original sin because she was to become the mother of his Son. The Immaculata was Saint Maximilian Kolbe's favorite name for the Blessed Mother.

9. **Knight**—in medieval times, a man, usually of noble birth, who was given an honorary military title by the king or by another high-ranking lord. Knights promised to observe a special code of conduct, which included the practice of courage, fairness, kindness, and a concern for the protection of the poor. Saint Maximilian considered himself and his friars knights in the service of Jesus and Mary.

10. **Minor seminary**—a high school whose purpose is to educate and prepare young men for the priesthood.

11. **Miraculous Medal**—the medal Saint Catherine Labouré had made and distributed at the request of the Blessed Mother, who appeared to her in Paris, France, in 1830.

This medal pictures Mary with her hands extended. Rays of light are coming from her hands. Around the image of Mary is printed the prayer, "O Mary, conceived without sin, pray for us who have recourse to you." The Miraculous Medal honors the mystery of Mary's Immaculate Conception.

12. **Monastery**—the place where friars, monks or nuns live as a community, dedicating themselves to a life of prayer.

13. **Novena**—nine days of prayer for some special need or occasion. This custom recalls the time that Mary and the first disciples of Jesus spent praying together between the ascension of Jesus into heaven and the coming of the Holy Spirit on Pentecost.

14. **Novitiate**—a period of training that comes before the making of vows in religious life.

15. **Parish mission**—a special time of prayer and reflection celebrated by a parish faith community. Visiting priests are usually invited to preach on different topics, and the sacrament of Penance is made available to the people.

16. **Provincial superior**—the person who governs several houses of the same religious order or congregation within a specific territory. These several houses make up a province.

17. **Recreation**—a time of relaxation and enjoyment.

18. **Refectory**—the dining room of a monastery or convent.

19. **Sanatorium**—an institution for the care of the sick, especially one which specializes in the treatment of a specific disease, such as tuberculosis.

20. **Vow**—an important promise freely made to God. Members of religious orders or congregations make the vows of poverty, chastity and obedience. Perpetual vows are the final vows made in a religious community. They are a sign of one's desire to consecrate his or her whole life to God forever. A person makes perpetual vows as a religious after a testing period of at least three years.

Who are the Daughters of St. Paul?

We are Catholic sisters. Our mission is to be like Saint Paul and tell everyone about Jesus! There are so many ways for people to communicate with each other. We want to use all of them so everyone will know how much God loves them. We do this by printing books (you're holding one!), making radio shows, singing, helping people at our bookstores, using the Internet, and in many other ways.

Visit our website at www.pauline.org

BOOKS & MEDIA

The Daughters of St. Paul operate book and media
centers at the following addresses. Visit, call, or write
the one nearest you today, or find us at www.pauline.org.

CALIFORNIA

3908 Sepulveda Blvd, Culver City, CA 90230   310-397-8676
935 Brewster Avenue, Redwood City, CA 94063   650-369-4230
5945 Balboa Avenue, San Diego, CA 92111   858-565-9181

FLORIDA

145 SW 107th Avenue, Miami, FL 33174   305-559-6715

HAWAII

1143 Bishop Street, Honolulu, HI 96813   808-521-2731

ILLINOIS

172 North Michigan Avenue, Chicago, IL 60601   312-346-4228

LOUISIANA

4403 Veterans Memorial Blvd, Metairie, LA 70006   504-887-7631

MASSACHUSETTS

885 Providence Hwy, Dedham, MA 02026   781-326-5385

MISSOURI

9804 Watson Road, St. Louis, MO 63126   314-965-3512

NEW YORK

64 West 38th Street, New York, NY 10018   212-754-1110

SOUTH CAROLINA

243 King Street, Charleston, SC 29401   843-577-0175

TEXAS

Currently no book center; for parish exhibits or outreach evangelization,
contact: 210-569-0500 or SanAntonio@paulinemedia.com

VIRGINIA

1025 King Street, Alexandria, VA 22314   703-549-3806

CANADA

3022 Dufferin Street, Toronto, ON M6B 3T5   416-781-9131